Love Came Down at Christmas

D0448725

©2013 by Barbour Publishing, Inc.

Print ISBN 978-1-62416-141-4

eBook Editions:
Adobe Digital Edition (epub) 978-1-62416-487-3
Kindle and MobiPocket Edition (prc) 978-1-62416-486-6

All rights reserved. No part of this publication may be reproduced or transmitted for commercial purposes, except for brief quotations in printed reviews, without written permission of the publisher.

Churches and other noncommercial interests may reproduce portions of this book without the express written permission of Barbour Publishing, provided that the text does not exceed 500 words or 5 percent of the entire book, whichever is less, and that the text is not material quoted from another publisher. When reproducing text from this book, include the following credit line: "From *Love Came Down at Christmas: A Celebration of Jesus' Birth*, published by Barbour Publishing, Inc. Used by permission."

All scripture quotations, unless otherwise indicated, are taken from the HOLY BIBLE, NEW INTERNATIONAL VERSION®. NIV®. Copyright © 1973, 1978, 1984, 2011 by Biblica, Inc.™ Used by permission. All rights reserved worldwide.

Scripture quotations marked NLT are taken from the *Holy Bible*. New Living Translation copyright© 1996, 2004, 2007 by Tyndale House Foundation. Used by permission of Tyndale House Publishers, Inc. Carol Stream, Illinois 60188. All rights reserved.

Scripture quotations marked ESV are from The Holy Bible, English Standard Version®, copyright © 2001 by Crossway Bibles, a publishing ministry of Good News Publishers. Used by permission. All rights reserved.

Cover design: Greg Jackson, Thinkpen Design

Published by Barbour Publishing, Inc., P.O. Box 719, Uhrichsville, Ohio 44683, www.barbourbooks.com

Our mission is to publish and distribute inspirational products offering exceptional value and biblical encouragement to the masses.

Member of the
Evangelical Christian
Publishers Association

Printed in China.

Love Came Down

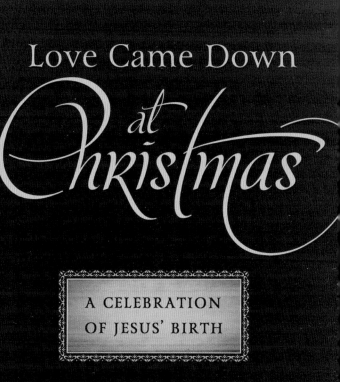

at Christmas

A CELEBRATION OF JESUS' BIRTH

MariLee Parrish

BARBOUR
PUBLISHING

Contents

It's Christmas here at the Parrish house, and the other evening I asked my five-year-old what we should give Jesus for Christmas. In years past, he has said, "Doughnuts!" (because everyone should have a doughnut on their birthday!), but this time he said we should give Jesus "a great big THANK YOU for dying on the cross for us!"

My little boy has figured out exactly what Jesus wants from us for Christmas—and for always.

Love came down at Christmas. He chose to come. He *chose* to die. He chose to save us. This is the good news of great joy that will be for all the people! And now we can spend our whole lives—and all eternity—giving Jesus a great big THANK YOU for what He has done.

Journey with me through Rossetti's timeless poem as we discover God's plan for Christmas.

Many Christmas Blessings,
MariLee Parrish

Love Came Down at Christmas

Love came down at Christmas,
Love all lovely, Love Divine,
Love was born at Christmas,
Star and Angels gave the sign.

Worship we the Godhead,
Love Incarnate, Love Divine,
Worship we our Jesus,
But wherewith for sacred sign?

Love shall be our token,
Love shall be yours and love be mine,
Love to God and all men,
Love for plea and gift and sign.

CHRISTINA ROSSETTI, 1893

Love Came Down

Love Came Down

❧

Whoever does not love
does not know God,
because God is love.
This is how God showed
his love among us:
He sent his one and only Son
into the world that we
might live through him.

1 JOHN 4:8–9

When God sent Jesus to earth, He sent *hope* and *love* and *life*! Many of us learn the John 3:16 "For God so loved the world" verse very early in life, but we often skip right past the ever important John 3:17. God's Word tells us that we can have eternal life by believing in Christ (John 3:16), and it goes on to say that God *did not* send Jesus to *condemn* the world but to *save* it! Religion and rules have brought shame and condemnation. But Jesus came to love and save. Don't allow Christmas to be just another religious tradition. Open your heart and let the real meaning of Christmas change you. Love came down at Christmas—real love! This Christmas, come to know the real Jesus. The baby in the manger grew up and took all our sin and shame upon Himself. Jesus conquered death with you and me on His mind and in His heart. Ask Him to be the center of your life and allow Him to fill you with His love. As evangelist and newspaper founder John R. Rice said, "You can never truly enjoy Christmas until you can look up into the Father's face and tell Him you have received His Christmas gift."

Love came down at Christmas.

Peace Came Down

❧

*And let the peace that comes from Christ rule in
your hearts. For as members of one body you are
called to live in peace. And always be thankful.*

COLOSSIANS 3:15 NLT

Early twentieth-century minister and college
professor W. J. Tucker said, "For centuries men
have kept an appointment with Christmas.
Christmas means fellowship, feasting, giving
and receiving, a time of good cheer, home."
While that thought may create a sense of joy
and excitement, it usually causes stress and
anxiety, too. Especially for the one hosting the
gathering! Fellowship, feasting, giving, home
also means shopping, cleaning, wrapping,
baking, and more. Christmas is a downright
exhausting time for some. The host wants
everything to be perfect, and the guests expect
holiday bliss. It can be a lot of pressure.

This Christmas, let the peace of the season
rule in your heart. As you prepare for your
Christmas gatherings, pray for the peace of

Christ to permeate your soul. Be thankful for friends and loved ones coming your way. Let them know in advance that while you'll still be creating some of the usual traditions, your focus will be more on the peace of Christmas and less on the hustle and bustle. Keep your family's appointment with Christmas but stop worrying about money and gifts and holiday perfection. Instead wrap your mind around the perfect Child born to bring peace to all mankind. While some may be a little disappointed that your meatballs came from the freezer section or the table placecards aren't hand-crafted, it's okay. You don't have to please everyone. In fact, you can't possibly please everyone! Concern yourself only with pleasing Christ. And He calls you to live in peace.

Peace came down at Christmas.

Infant holy, infant lowly,
for his bed a cattle stall;
oxen lowing, little knowing,
Christ the babe is Lord of all.
Swift are winging angels singing,
noels ringing, tidings bringing:
Christ the babe is Lord of all.

Flocks were sleeping,
shepherds keeping
vigil till the morning new
saw the glory, heard the story,
tidings of a Gospel true.
Thus rejoicing, free from sorrow,
praises voicing, greet the morrow:
Christ the babe was born for you.

POLISH CAROL

Love came down on Christmas Day
so many years ago and brought the
greatest happiness the world would
ever know... Peace came down on
Christmas Day to fill the hearts of
men with all the sweet tranquility each
Christmas brings again... Joy came
down on Christmas Day as angels
came to earth heralding the miracle
of our Messiah's birth.

UNKNOWN

Joy Came Down

❦

Though you have not seen him, you love him;
and even though you do not see him now,
you believe in him and are filled with
an inexpressible and glorious joy, for you
are receiving the end result of your faith,
the salvation of your souls.

1 PETER 1:8–9

On an economy that is struggling, in a country where nearly 50 percent of first-time marriages end in divorce, in a nation that permits the killing of the unborn and hurting people numb their feelings with any number of preoccupations—true joy is hard to come by. We have so much—yet our souls are filled with so little.

God chose to enter the world as an infant in a time of Roman oppression when earthly kings had the power to do whatever they liked, including having all the male babies under the age of two killed. People lived in fear and had little control over their own lives. People live in fear today, too. We may fear for different reasons, but fear is fear. The good news is that Jesus came to cast out all fear (1 John 4:18) and bring joy to the world.

Christian musician Michael Card said it well: "The implications of the name 'Immanuel' are both comforting and unsettling. Comforting, because He has come to share the danger as well as the drudgery of our everyday lives. He desires to weep with us and to wipe away our tears. And what seems most bizarre, Jesus Christ, the Son of God, longs to share in and to be the source of the laughter and the joy we all too rarely know."

Joy came down at Christmas.

Lord Jesus, master of both the light and the darkness, send Your Holy Spirit upon our preparations for Christmas. We who have so much to do seek quiet spaces to hear Your voice each day. We who are anxious over many things look forward to Your coming among us. We who are blessed in so many ways long for the complete joy of Your kingdom. We whose hearts are heavy seek the joy of Your presence. We are Your people, walking in darkness yet seeking the light. To You we say, "Come, Lord Jesus!" (*Prayer by Henri J. M. Nouwen*)

Oh Lord, let me love as You have loved. Show me how to live a life that pleases You and draws those around me to seek Your face. This Christmas, be my joy. Be my hope. Be the light that burns so fervently in my heart that everyone around me will know that You alone are God—and You are Love. Thank You for bringing inexpressible and glorious joy to this dark world. I never have to live in fear because You—perfect love—have come!

Hope Came Down

*May the God of hope fill
you with all joy and peace
as you trust in him,
so that you may overflow
with hope by the power
of the Holy Spirit.*

ROMANS 15:13

Jesus didn't have to come like He did or when He did. He chose to be born as a commoner. He chose to grow up with everyday people instead of in a palace as He deserved. He could have chosen to come now while lethal injection is the punishment for criminals instead of at a time when He would have to hang, nailed to a cross, with thorns piercing his head.

In Max Lucado's book *God Came Near*, Lucado reminds us that God had this choice in coming. He left heaven and chose to come because of us. Lucado writes, "Since he could bear your sins more easily than he could bear the thought of your hopelessness, he chose to leave [heaven]."

People were hopeless then and they are hopeless now. While Jesus chose to arrive in Bethlehem two thousand years ago, He offers the same hope to all today. He is the same yesterday, today, and forever (Hebrews 13:8). Jesus can look into any weary, dark, and hopeless soul and fill it with hope and a peace that transcends all understanding (Philippians 4:7) and every circumstance.

Hope came down at Christmas.

Love, Joy, and Peace

*But the Holy Spirit produces this kind of fruit
in our lives: love, joy, peace, patience, kindness,
goodness, faithfulness, gentleness, and self-control.
There is no law against these things! . . .
Since we are living by the Spirit, let us follow
the Spirit's leading in every part of our lives.*

GALATIANS 5:22–23, 25 NLT

The true spirit of Christmas is love, joy, and peace. If you think about your holiday shopping experience this season, is that the impression you get as you place your purchases on the checkout counter? Probably not. Even as Christians we get caught up in the crazy race of the season. We strive for perfection. The perfect tree. The perfect gifts. The perfect Christmas outfits and photo sessions and Christmas cards and cookie trays. . .

If Jesus walked into a big-box store this Christmas, what would He say to the frazzled mom carrying a fussy baby on her hip and pushing a cart full of presents she can't afford?

How would He react to the grumpy man complaining and cursing in the back of the line? What would He do if He was accidentally shoved by a group of people trying to get the very last carton of eggs on the shelf?

Jesus placed His love, joy, and peace in your heart, and He has you right where He wants you. As you are surrounded with commercialism and preoccupied people this Christmas, exhibit Jesus' love, joy, and peace to everyone you come in contact with. It is not an accident that you experience what you do. Don't think it odd that you seem to witness the strangest things. Think of it as a divine appointment and allow God to use you in every situation.

Love, joy, and peace came down at Christmas.

Though our feelings come and go,
God's love for us does not.

C. S. LEWIS

❧

It is good to be children
sometimes, and never better
than at Christmas, when its mighty
founder was a child Himself.

CHARLES DICKENS

❧

Nails didn't hold Him
on the cross. Love did!

MAX LUCADO

Jesus loves me! This I know,
For the Bible tells me so;
Little ones to Him belong,
They are weak but He is strong.

Yes, Jesus loves me!
Yes, Jesus loves me!
Yes, Jesus loves me!
The Bible tells me so.

Jesus loves me! He who died,
Heaven's gate to open wide;
He will wash away my sin,
Let His little child come in.

ANNA BARTLETT WARNER

Christmas in Your Heart

❧

*"Do not store up for yourselves treasures
on earth, where moths and vermin destroy,
and where thieves break in and steal. But store up
for yourselves treasures in heaven, where moths
and vermin do not destroy, and where thieves
do not break in and steal. For where your
treasure is, there your heart will be also."*

MATTHEW 6:19–21

The song "Looking for Love in All the Wrong
Places" comes to mind when considering the
consumer's mad rush to find a perfect gift.
Gifts certainly aren't bad things, but we tend
to use them because we don't know how to
truly express our love to those closest to us.
You can't just find Christmas under a tree. As
clergyman Roy L. Smith so aptly put it, "He
who has not Christmas in his heart will never
find it under a tree."

The truth is that a mother would rather
have a picture colored by her preschooler, a
wife would rather have a heartfelt love letter

from her beloved husband, and a grandfather would rather have a home-cooked meal and the presence of his family rather than any present you could ever buy. Those heartfelt gifts cost next to nothing. . .and mean nearly everything to the recipient.

This Christmas, challenge your family to give heartfelt gifts to one another. Check your records and find out what you've spent during holidays past. Give everyone a spending limit and decide as a family to give the difference to your church or to a charitable organization. You don't need to spend a lot of money to make your loved ones happy. The gift of your presence—not presents—and true words of love are enough to make any heart glad.

Christmas is all about You, Jesus. Perfect love came down at Christmas. Remind me of Your purpose and Your presence as I head into this holiday season. I confess that my priorities get messed up sometimes. And my family looks more at material things than eternal things. Please change that for us. Help us be givers— but not just of material things. Help us give of ourselves and to give and show love. Open our eyes and our hearts this season.

This Christmas, Lord, help me store up treasures in heaven and not worry so much about material things. Help my family get on board with this idea, too. Give us eternal perspectives as we use the money and gifts You have given us. Thank You for giving us true and lasting joy that only comes from a personal relationship with You. Be the center of our Christmas—and the center of our everyday lives. Help us honor You with every decision we make.

*Love All Lovely,
Love Divine*

Divine Love

❧

For I am convinced that neither death nor life,
neither angels nor demons, neither the present
nor the future, nor any powers, neither height
nor depth, nor anything else in all creation,
will be able to separate us from the love of
God that is in Christ Jesus our Lord.

ROMANS 8:38–39

"For God so loved the world". . . That's really the whole point of Christmas. Saint Augustine said, "Nothing was so necessary for raising our hope as to show us how deeply God loved us. And what could afford us a stronger proof of this than that the Son of God should become a partner with us of human nature?" God became one of us. Fully human and yet somehow fully God.

And He gave each of us a choice from the very beginning. Yes, He could have created us as robots programmed to love and never sin. But what kind of love would that be? How could anyone have a personal, meaningful relationship with a piece of semi-intelligent software? God wanted us to choose to love Him back. Mankind messed up though. We all sin and fall short of God's glory (Romans 3:23). The Bible tells us that the price of sin is death, because God is holy and demands nothing less.

That's where Jesus comes in. God loves each of us so much He couldn't leave us without hope. He sent our Savior to take our place so that nothing can separate us from God's love—ever! And now "the gift of God is eternal life in Christ Jesus our Lord" (Romans 6:23).

Christmas is the beginning of that free gift. Divine love in the flesh.

The Greatest Gift

❧

But because of his great love for us,
God, who is rich in mercy, made us
alive with Christ even when we were
dead in transgressions— it is by
grace you have been saved.

EPHESIANS 2:4–5 NIV

Have you accepted God's Christmas gift? The Bible tells us that it's not enough to just believe there is a God. Even the demons believe in God (James 2:19). Instead, we must accept Jesus as our Lord and Savior, a baby born to give us eternal life and a place among God's family. John 1:12 says, "To all who did receive him, to those who believed in his name, he gave the right to become children of God."

C. S. Lewis put it this way: "The Son of God became a man to enable men to become the sons of God." God is waiting for each of us to accept His Christmas gift. "Here I am!" He declares, "I stand at the door and knock. If anyone hears my voice and opens the door, I will come in" (Revelation 3:20).

God is standing at the door of our hearts, waiting to make us His children. If you've never accepted His free gift of eternal life through Jesus, quiet your heart before Him now and allow Him to give you the greatest gift of all. First John 1:9 says, "If we confess our sins, he is faithful and just and will forgive us our sins and purify us from all unrighteousness." Open your heart and talk to God. He loves you so much and wants to clear your conscience and take away all your sins.

Invite Him in this Christmas.

Love divine, all loves excelling,
Joy of heaven to earth come down;
Fix in us thy humble dwelling;
All thy faithful mercies crown!
Jesus, Thou art all compassion,
Pure unbounded love Thou art;
Visit us with Thy salvation;
Enter every trembling heart.

Come, Almighty to deliver,
Let us all Thy life receive;
Suddenly return and never,
Never more Thy temples leave.
Thee we would be always blessing,
Serve Thee as Thy hosts above,
Pray and praise Thee without ceasing,
Glory in Thy perfect love.

CHARLES WESLEY

The hinge of history is on the
door of a Bethlehem stable.

RALPH W. SOCKMAN

Take Christ out of Christmas,
and December becomes the bleakest
and most colorless month of the year.

A. F. WELLS

Heavenly Father, I do not deserve Your divine love. I've messed up so much. I've chosen my way so many times, knowing that You are calling to me to come and follow You. I'm tired of making wrong choices. I'm disgusted by the mess I've made of my life. Will you come and clean my soul? Forgive me for the choices I've made. I choose You now. I hear You knocking, and I'm inviting You in this Christmas. Change my life and make me a new person. I accept the free gift of eternal life through Your Son, Jesus.

Jesus, thank You for choosing to come like You did. Your love for me is amazing. I often read about Your life in the Bible and what You went through for me on the cross, and it just seems inconceivable. Yet my heart tells me it's true. Words aren't enough to thank You or tell You how this makes me feel. I'll do my best to live for You each and every day so that my whole life will be a "thank You!"

The Presence of Christ

*"The Lord your God is with you, the Mighty
Warrior who saves. He will take great delight
in you; in his love he will no longer rebuke you,
but will rejoice over you with singing."*

ZEPHANIAH 3:17

Author and pastor Dr. David Jeremiah
said, "All the Christmas presents in the world
are worth nothing without the presence of
Christ." If you haven't accepted God's gift
to you, no amount of shopping or searching
elsewhere will fill the emptiness and longing in
your heart. Many of us have already accepted
Christ, though, but have allowed the demands
of life and family to crowd out a relationship
with God. We believe in God; we've trusted
Christ as our Savior; but the sparkle that once
lit our eyes has been replaced by stress and
everyday busyness.

As you go about your holiday preparations,
stop long enough to remember that God is
with you. Ask Him to quiet you with His love.

Ask Him to rearrange your life to match His plans and purposes. Remember, He *delights* in you! He actually sings over you!

Colossians 3:1–2 says, "Since, then, you have been raised with Christ, set your hearts on things above, where Christ is, seated at the right hand of God. Set your minds on things above, not on earthly things." As hard as it may be to set your heart on eternal things this Christmas instead of the hustle and bustle, the Spirit of God is with you and will help you do His will if you let Him.

Keep Christmas Well

❧

*Dear friends, let us continue to love
one another, for love comes from God.
Anyone who loves is a child of God and
knows God. But anyone who does not
love does not know God, for God is love.*

1 JOHN 4:7–8 NLT

Most of us know the story of Ebenezer Scrooge in Charles Dickens's *A Christmas Carol*. Yet, year after year, we love to watch the grumpy, cheerless man become a lover of Christmas. Scrooge was so drastically changed by the end that "it was always said of him, that he knew how to keep Christmas well."

Divine love will do that to a person. The love of God indwelling inside mankind is absolutely life-changing. Most people think of love as a feeling, when in reality, love is a choice and an action. Feelings will come and go, but love is always a choice.

Keeping Christmas well involves choosing to love God and others on a moment-by-moment basis and then acting on that decision. Are you keeping Christmas well the whole year through? Ask God to fill you with His divine love and give you the desire to choose love every day.

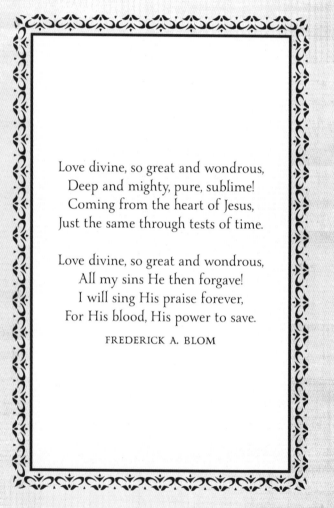

Love divine, so great and wondrous,
Deep and mighty, pure, sublime!
Coming from the heart of Jesus,
Just the same through tests of time.

Love divine, so great and wondrous,
All my sins He then forgave!
I will sing His praise forever,
For His blood, His power to save.

FREDERICK A. BLOM

I truly believe that if we keep telling the Christmas story, singing the Christmas songs, and living the Christmas spirit, we can bring joy and happiness and peace to this world.

NORMAN VINCENT PEALE

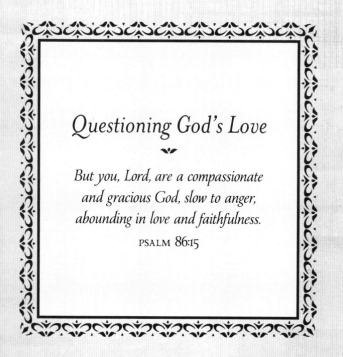

Questioning God's Love

*But you, Lord, are a compassionate
and gracious God, slow to anger,
abounding in love and faithfulness.*

PSALM 86:15

Whenever you question God's love for you,
remember what Jesus did on the cross. And
allow the following verses to transform your
thoughts:

The LORD is compassionate and gracious,
slow to anger, abounding in love.
He will not always accuse,
nor will he harbor his anger forever;
he does not treat us as our sins deserve
or repay us according to our iniquities.
For as high as the heavens are above the earth,
so great is his love for those who fear him;
as far as the east is from the west,
so far has he removed our transgressions from us.
As a father has compassion on his children,
so the LORD has compassion on those who fear him.

PSALM 103:8–13

God is slow to anger and abounding in love, and that is a message worth repeating. You will find this same message if you look up Exodus 34:6, Numbers 14:18, Nehemiah 9:17, Psalm 145:8, Joel 2:13, Jonah 4:2, and Nahum 1:3. Whenever you're wondering if God is mad at you or if your feelings are getting in the way of the truth from God's Word, take time to look up these verses and let them soak into your heart.

Heavenly Father, as I prepare for the holidays this year, help me remember that You are always with me. Quiet me with Your love. Allow the stress to melt away as I worship You. I know I'm too busy. Help me rearrange my life to match Your plans and purposes. It's all about You, Jesus. There are days when I forget this and I try to force things to go my way. Help me relax and enjoy the situations You've placed me in.

Lord, I ask that You fill me with Your divine love. Please give me the desire to choose love every day. Sometimes I don't feel like loving others. And I feel unlovable myself, at times. Allow the Holy Spirit to remind me of the scriptures that tell me that You are slow to anger and abounding in love. Help me choose love even when I don't feel like it.

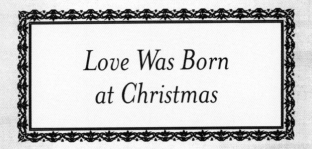

Love Was Born
at Christmas

Love Was Born
at Christmas

❧

"Joseph son of David, do not be afraid to take Mary home as your wife, because what is conceived in her is from the Holy Spirit. She will give birth to a son, and you are to give him the name Jesus, because he will save his people from their sins."

MATTHEW 1:20–21

In Hebrew, the name Jesus is *Yeshua*, which means "the Lord (Yahweh) saves." First John 4:10 explains, "This is love: not that we loved God, but that he loved us and sent his Son as an atoning sacrifice for our sins." God's plan was to send Jesus—Himself in the flesh—to earth to show us what real love was. And so love was born at Christmas. Divine love. Real love. Perfect love. Saving love.

German pastor Dietrich Bonhoeffer, who was hanged by the Nazis in 1945, said, "A prison cell, in which one waits, hopes. . .and is completely dependent on the fact that the door of freedom has to be opened from the outside, is not a bad picture of Advent." Jesus came to save people from their sins. And we are completely dependent on the fact that *only* Jesus can save us. Without His work on the cross, we are hopeless. With it, we are victorious.

But it all started when an angel appeared to Mary in a small town thousands of years ago. She waited and hoped. And what was promised to her came true for all people.

God with Us

❧

All this took place to fulfill what the Lord
had said through the prophet: "The virgin
will conceive and give birth to a son,
and they will call him Immanuel"
(which means, "God with us").

MATTHEW 1:22–23

Author and pastor John F. MacArthur Jr.
said, "If we could condense all the truths of
Christmas into only three words, these would
be the words: 'God with us.' We tend to focus
our attention at Christmas on the infancy of
Christ. The greater truth of the holiday is His
deity. More astonishing than a baby in the

manger is the truth that this promised baby is the omnipotent Creator of the heavens and the earth!"

Don't let the Christ of Christmas stay in the manger. Let Him grow up and mature in you. Allow the power of the Holy Spirit to do miracles in your own heart. Sure, thinking of Him as a baby is much sweeter and more palatable than the actual truth of His perfect life and gruesome death. In fact, millions of people accept Jesus as an historic figure only. They believe that Jesus was a moral teacher, born in a stable, who grew up to be a great leader. Men, women, and children across the world will gaze at a live nativity scene as if it were a simple, peaceful symbol of the season, unaware—or choosing to overlook—Jesus' great sacrifice for all mankind.

But Jesus isn't just another symbol of the season. That miraculous baby grew up with one mission: to die on a cross and save us from our sins. His resurrection and return to heaven allowed the Holy Spirit (John 16:7) to indwell in all believers' hearts so that we can forever have "God with us."

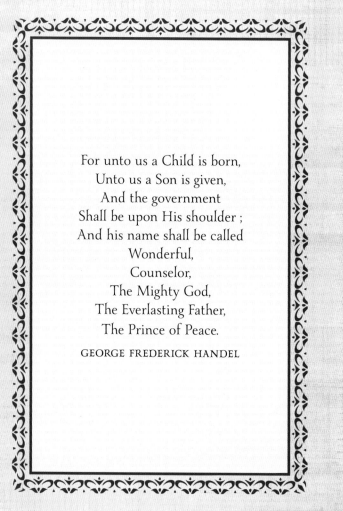

For unto us a Child is born,
Unto us a Son is given,
And the government
Shall be upon His shoulder ;
And his name shall be called
Wonderful,
Counselor,
The Mighty God,
The Everlasting Father,
The Prince of Peace.

GEORGE FREDERICK HANDEL

It is Christmas in the heart
that puts Christmas in the air.

W. T. ELLIS

No Room

All returned to their own ancestral towns to register for this census. And because Joseph was a descendant of King David, he had to go to Bethlehem in Judea, David's ancient home. He traveled there from the village of Nazareth in Galilee. He took with him Mary, his fiancée, who was now obviously pregnant. And while they were there, the time came for her baby to be born. She gave birth to her first child, a son. She wrapped him snugly in strips of cloth and laid him in a manger, because there was no lodging available for them.

LUKE 2:3–7 NLT

*E*vangelist Billy Graham said, "One response was given by the innkeeper when Mary and Joseph wanted to find a room where the Child could be born. The innkeeper was not hostile; he was not opposed to them, but his inn was crowded; his hands were full; his mind was preoccupied. This is the answer that millions are giving today. Like a Bethlehem innkeeper, they cannot find room for Christ. All the accommodations in their hearts are already taken up by other crowding interests. Their response is not atheism. It is not defiance. It is preoccupation and the feeling of being able to get on reasonably well without Christianity."

Think of your family and friends. Maybe one or two of them is adamantly opposed to God and deny His very existence, but most probably do believe there is a God. In fact, they even pay tribute to Him on Christmas and Easter. But the rest of the year they are too preoccupied with other interests to hear what God has to say to them. There is no room in their lives for God.

As you visit with friends and family this holiday season, pray specifically for those you come in contact with, that they will make room in their hearts and lives for God. Ask Him to use you as an example of what that looks like.

Heavenly Father, thank You for sending Your Son at Christmas. As we celebrate His birth, I am in awe of His purpose in life: to save us! To be the Way, the Truth, and the Life. To be our complete access to You. It is so amazing to me that You care about me personally and want to be with me for all eternity. Thank You for Jesus. Thank You for showing me what real love is.

Lord Jesus, help me see You as You really are. Not just a symbol of the season, not just a baby in the manger, but everlasting life. The love of God in the flesh. Please give me an eternal perspective about everything that happens to me here in this world. Allow the power of the Holy Spirit to transform me and do miracles in my heart. I pray for my family and friends. Help them make room in their hearts for You. Let me be an example of what a life transformed by Your love looks like.

Heaven and Nature Sing

❧

And there were shepherds living out in the fields nearby, keeping watch over their flocks at night. An angel of the Lord appeared to them, and the glory of the Lord shone around them, and they were terrified. But the angel said to them, "Do not be afraid. I bring you good news that will cause great joy for all the people. Today in the town of David a Savior has been born to you; he is the Messiah, the Lord. This will be a sign to you: You will find a baby wrapped in cloths and lying in a manger."

LUKE 2:8–12

The late writer and monk Thomas Merton said, "There were only a few shepherds at the first Bethlehem. The ox and the donkey understood more of the first Christmas than the high priests in Jerusalem. And it is the same today."

Consider this excerpt from Psalm 148:

Praise him, sun and moon; praise him, all you shining stars. . . . Let them praise the name of the LORD, for at his command they were created and he established them for ever and ever—he issued a decree that will never pass away. Praise the LORD from the earth. . .wild animals and all cattle, small creatures and flying birds. . . . Let them praise the name of the LORD, for his name alone is exalted; his splendor is above the earth and the heavens.

Love was born. Heaven and nature sang. The rocks cried out. Even the animals understood that a King was born! We humans have gone to great lengths to disprove God when all creation around us is screaming: "God is real! God did this! This is the good news of great joy for all the people! A savior has been born."

Peace to Mankind

❦

Suddenly a great company of the heavenly host appeared with the angel, praising God and saying, "Glory to God in the highest heaven, and on earth peace to those on whom his favor rests."

LUKE 2:13–14

While God was forming our hearts, the Bible tells us that He set eternity right there inside (Ecclesiastes 3:11). So as long as we live, we will never be made whole until we have made peace with our Creator. Until we've accepted His love and begin to live out a daily relationship with Him.

The peace God gives is beyond our understanding (Philippians 4:6–7). In the middle of grief, trouble, suffering, stress, and the messes we get ourselves into, God offers hope. We can know His peace that comes through a relationship with Him in Christ: "He is before all things, and in him all things hold together. And he is the head of the body, the church; he is the beginning and the firstborn from among the dead, so that in everything he might have the supremacy. For God was pleased to have all his fullness dwell in him, and through him to reconcile to himself all things, whether things on earth or things in heaven, by making peace through his blood, shed on the cross" (Colossians 1:17-20).

God sent Jesus—to be born in a stable, to grow up and live a perfect life, to die on a cross—to bring us peace. As author and Holocaust survivor Corrie ten Boom put it, "Who can add to Christmas? The perfect motive is that God so loved the world. The perfect gift is that He gave His only Son. The only requirement is to believe in Him. The reward of faith is that you shall have everlasting life."

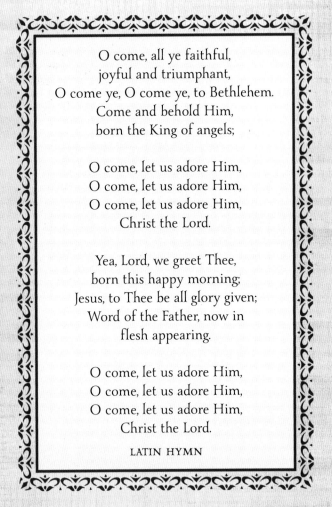

O come, all ye faithful,
joyful and triumphant,
O come ye, O come ye, to Bethlehem.
Come and behold Him,
born the King of angels;

O come, let us adore Him,
O come, let us adore Him,
O come, let us adore Him,
Christ the Lord.

Yea, Lord, we greet Thee,
born this happy morning;
Jesus, to Thee be all glory given;
Word of the Father, now in
flesh appearing.

O come, let us adore Him,
O come, let us adore Him,
O come, let us adore Him,
Christ the Lord.

LATIN HYMN

Off to one side sits a group of shepherds.
They sit silently on the floor, perhaps perplexed,
perhaps in awe, no doubt in amazement.
Their night watch had been interrupted by an
explosion of light from heaven and a symphony
of angels. God goes to those who have time
to hear Him—and so on this cloudless night
He went to simple shepherds.

MAX LUCADO

Do the Next Thing

❦

When the angels had left them and gone into heaven, the shepherds said to one another, "Let's go to Bethlehem and see this thing that has happened, which the Lord has told us about." So they hurried off and found Mary and Joseph, and the baby, who was lying in the manger. When they had seen him, they spread the word concerning what had been told them about this child, and all who heard it were amazed at what the shepherds said to them.

LUKE 2:15–18

The Bible tells us that the shepherds were terrified. They were everyday guys just doing their job when they were visited by angels. What is your response when you are terrified? Are you paralyzed by your fear?

An old Saxon poem called "Doe the Nexte Thynge" (Do the Next Thing) reads:

Fear not tomorrows, child of the King,
Trust them with Jesus, doe the nexte thynge.
Do it immediately, do it with prayer;
Do it reliantly, casting all care;
Do it with reverence, tracing His hand
Who placed it before thee with earnest command.
Stayed on Omnipotence, safe 'neath His wing,
Leave all resulting, doe the nexte thynge.

Whenever fear threatens to take over, set your feelings aside and trust the faithfulness of God. Like the shepherds, do what God is telling you to do. Do it immediately and do it with prayer. Remember, His perfect love will cast out your fear (1 John 4:18).

I praise the name of the Lord. Your name alone is exalted. Your splendor is everywhere. Your whole creation sings Your praise. Even the animals know of Your greatness. Thank You for making Your love plain to me. It is clear that You alone are God. I come and adore You, Christ the Lord. Father, help me put a halt on things. With all the plans and activities in place, I feel like this Christmas has already gotten out of control. Help me slow down and truly adore You this Christmas—and always.

Father, I praise You for offering hope and peace in the middle of grief, trouble, suffering, stress, and the messes I get myself into. I want to know Your peace fully. The peace that comes from a day-to-day relationship with You. When I am afraid, help me trust You. Give me the ability to set my feelings aside and trust in Your faithfulness. Like the shepherds, help me do what You tell me to, even when I'm afraid. I want to follow You all the days of my life.

Star and Angels
Gave the Sign

The Wise Men and the Star

❦

*After Jesus was born in Bethlehem in Judea,
during the time of King Herod, Magi from
the east came to Jerusalem and asked,
"Where is the one who has been born
king of the Jews? We saw his star when
it rose and have come to worship him."*

MATTHEW 2:1

The wise men, or Magi, are generally found
in nativity scenes and depictions of the birth
of Christ. But the Magi did not arrive the night
Jesus was born. The Bible tells us that Jesus was
a bit older and living in a house when the Magi
came. We don't know a lot about these wise
men, but we do know that they saw a special

star and somehow understood it was the star that would lead them to Jesus, the King.

Author and pastor Dr. D. James Kennedy said, "The star of Bethlehem was a star of hope that led the wise men to the fulfillment of their expectations, the success of their expedition. Nothing in this world is more fundamental for success in life than hope, and this star pointed to our only source for true hope: Jesus Christ."

The message of that first star continues through the ages. Psalm 8:3-5 says, "When I look at the night sky and see the work of your fingers—the moon and the stars you set in place—what are mere mortals that you should think about them, human beings that you should care about them? Yet you made them only a little lower than God and crowned them with glory and honor" (NLT).

God the Father set a special star in place that would lead wise men to seek Jesus. His creation calls to wise men and women still: "I care for you. I love you. Come and follow me."

A Shepherd Was Born

❧

*When he had called together all the people's
chief priests and teachers of the law, he
asked them where the Messiah was to be
born. "In Bethlehem in Judea," they replied,
"for this is what the prophet has written:
'But you, Bethlehem, in the land of Judah,
are by no means least among the rulers
of Judah; for out of you will come a ruler
who will shepherd my people Israel.'"*

MATTHEW 2:4–6

Jesus was born at a time when tyrants were kings. Most used their power for evil instead of good. King Herod, who was ruler at the time when the wise men were looking for Jesus, murdered many of his own family. Rulers were dictating bullies. So to hear that a ruler would come who would be a "shepherd of the people" was quite contrary to the status quo.

This shepherd is One who calls gently to each of His sheep: "Do not be afraid, little flock, for your Father has been pleased to give you the kingdom" (Luke 12:32); "My sheep listen to my voice; I know them, and they follow me. I give them eternal life, and they shall never perish; no one can snatch them out of my hand" (John 10:27-28).

Can you hear the care and love resounding in His voice? Jesus, the King of kings, is not a tyrant ruler but a gentle shepherd. Listen as He gently calls your name.

As with gladness, men of old
Did the guiding star behold;
As with joy they hailed its light
Leading onward, beaming bright,
So, most glorious Lord, may we
Evermore be led to Thee.

Holy Jesus, every day
Keep us in the narrow way;
And, when earthly things are past,
Bring our ransomed souls at last
Where they need no star to guide,
Where no clouds Thy glory hide. . . .

In the heavenly country bright,
Need they no created light;
Thou its Light, its Joy, its Crown,
Thou its Sun which goes not down;
There forever may we sing
Alleluias to our King!

WILLIAM C. DIX

Lord Jesus, I see a lot of stars and angels popping up everywhere in storefront window displays, house decorations, and even on my own tree. Help me remember what these decorations represent. Christmas is so much more than pretty decorations and twinkling stars and lights. It's all about You, Jesus. Let Your light shine through me so that others can see that You are real and that You are working in my heart. Father, let all that I do please You today. Help me keep my focus on the true meaning of Christmas.

Heavenly Father, I worship You for
sending Your Son into the world to save me
from my sins so that I can be with You forever.
Thank You for calling me to be Your child.
I am so thankful that You love me and take
care of me. You are my gentle shepherd,
and I listen for Your voice. Help me set my
heart and my mind on You today and always.
Help me not only to share my faith with
all of those around me this Christmas
but to live out my faith each day.

Tired and Weary Travelers

❧

*After they had heard the king, they went
on their way, and the star they had seen
when it rose went ahead of them until it
stopped over the place where the child was.
When they saw the star, they were overjoyed.*

MATTHEW 2:9–10

The wise men had to be tired from following
the star that would lead to Jesus. They were
from another country, but they knew this baby
was worthy of their worship. First they went
to King Herod to find Jesus' whereabouts; then
they had to wait while Herod called together
all his chief priests and teachers to get more in-
formation. Finally the king sent them on their
way. The Bible tells us they were overjoyed
when they saw the star that had stopped over
the place where Jesus was.

French mathematician and Christian
philosopher Blaise Pascal said, "It is good to be
tired and wearied by the futile search after the
true good, that we may stretch out our arms to

the Redeemer." Doesn't that remind you of the wise men? When they saw Jesus' star, they were so happy to have concluded their search. They found their King.

Are you tired and wearied by your search for things that have no meaning? Or maybe you're just tired of all the running around and you want this Christmas to be a little bit different. In Matthew 11:28, Jesus tells us, "Come to me, all you who are weary and burdened, and I will give you rest."

Stretch out your arms to the Redeemer and rest in Him. Let this Christmas be different from all the others.

God's Great Gift-Giving

On coming to the house, they saw the child with his mother Mary, and they bowed down and worshiped him. Then they opened their treasures and presented him with gifts of gold, frankincense and myrrh. And having been warned in a dream not to go back to Herod, they returned to their country by another route.

MATTHEW 2:11–12

The very first Christmas gifts are listed in the Bible: gold, incense, and myrrh. If you've grown up in the church, you've probably heard about these gifts every Christmas. But what do they really mean?

Gold, frankincense, and myrrh were traditional gifts given to royalty. However, these gifts may also have had deeper spiritual meaning. Scholars say that gold was given to symbolize Jesus' kingship here on earth. Frankincense symbolized the deity of the Christ child, and myrrh typically was used for embalming. So the special gifts from the Magi could have meant that Jesus was a king, that He was God, and that He was going to die. Does it make you wonder what Mary felt as she accepted these gifts for her child?

Whatever the gifts symbolized, the wise men brought them in worship. They, educated as they were, bowed down before this small child and offered Him their adoration. They understood that this child was not what He appeared. This baby was God's great gift to all mankind.

Sleep, my child, and peace attend thee
All through the night.
Guardian angels God will send thee
All through the night.

Soft the drowsy hours are creeping,
Hill and vale in slumber sleeping,
Mother dear, her watch is keeping,
All through the night. . . .

God is here, thou'lt not be lonely
All through the night.
'Tis not I who guards thee only
All through the night.

Night's dark shades will soon be over;
Still my watchful care shall hover.
God with me His watch is keeping
All through the night.

TRADITIONAL WELSH FOLK SONG

God Is Light

❦

*This is the message we heard from Jesus
and now declare to you: God is light,
and there is no darkness in him at all.
So we are lying if we say we have fellowship with God but go on living in spiritual
darkness; we are not practicing the truth.
But if we are living in the light, as God is
in the light, then we have fellowship with
each other, and the blood of Jesus, his Son,
cleanses us from all sin.*

1 JOHN 1:5–7 NLT

Author Lenora Mattingly Weber said, "Christmas is for children. But it is for grown-ups, too. Even if it is a headache, a chore, and nightmare, it is a period of necessary defrosting of chill and hide-bound hearts." Weber's words are sad and true in many ways. We are the ones that make Christmas a headache, a chore, and a nightmare by getting caught up with commercialism and perfection. The enemy loves to get us so busy and focused on those two issues that we forget Christmas's true meaning. But, as Weber states, it is also a "necessary defrosting of chill." Families come together on Christmas. Hearts soften just a little in even the gruffest of individuals. Christmas means something. And most people know it. Even if they don't understand the true meaning.

This year, as you admire the twinkling beauty of Christmas lights, ask the Lord to continually light up your heart with His love. Confess your sins to Him and get rid of any darkness that might be invading your soul. Allow the light of Christ to defrost the chill in your heart, and pray that He does the same for those around you.

Jesus, I hear You saying, "Come to me, all you who are weary and burdened, and I will give you rest" (Matthew 11:28). I'm in need of rest. I want to celebrate *You* this Christmas and to slow down with everything else that doesn't really matter. I'm tired and weary. I'm pursuing things that add stress and take away time with You and my family. Please let this Christmas be different. I'm stretching out my arms to You, my Redeemer. May this Christmas be pleasing to You.

Dear God, please purify my heart and remove all of the darkness within me. Let Your light shine in my soul so that others may see You living in me. Defrost my heart. Warm me up inside. Help me live in the light as You are in the light. Keep me from all darkness. I pray the same for my friends and family. Use me in my relationships. Soften my friends' hearts and allow me opportunities to share Your light and love.

Love Incarnate,
Love Divine

Incarnation

❧

In the beginning was the Word, and the Word was
with God, and the Word was God. He was with
God in the beginning. Through him all things were
made; without him nothing was made that has
been made. In him was life, and that life was the
light of all mankind. The light shines in the
darkness, and the darkness has not overcome it.

JOHN 1:1–5

Christmas is all about the incarnation. God
becoming man and living as one of us. As
Oswald Chambers put it, "Jesus Christ became
incarnate for one purpose, to make a way back
to God that man might stand before Him as
he was created to do, the friend and lover of
God Himself." When Jesus became human, He
never stopped being God. "The Son is the image of the invisible God, the firstborn over all
creation" (Colossians 1:15).

The whole point is this: "Once you were
alienated from God and were enemies in your

minds because of your evil behavior. But now he has reconciled you by Christ's physical body through death to present you holy in his sight, without blemish and free from accusation" (Colossians 1:21–22).

The incarnation makes us free from accusation. We can stand before God as His friend, holy in His sight because of Jesus' birth, life, death, and resurrection. Love incarnate, love divine. In Him is life everlasting, the light of all mankind. Christmas is a celebration of the incarnation.

God Became Flesh

❧

*The Word became flesh and made
his dwelling among us. We have seen
his glory, the glory of the one and
only Son, who came from the Father,
full of grace and truth.*

JOHN 1:14

John 1:14–one of the most profound and
overwhelming truths in scripture. God became
flesh and came to dwell with us on earth.
Theologian and author J. I. Packer said, "It is
here, in the thing that happened at the first
Christmas, that the most profound unfathom-
able depths of the Christian revelation lie. God

became man...the Almighty appeared on earth as a helpless human baby, unable to do more than lie and stare and wriggle and make noises, needing to be fed and changed and taught to talk like any other child.... The more you think about it, the more staggering it gets. Nothing in fiction is so fantastic as this truth of the incarnation."

Ponder that for a moment. God—the creator of all things—made Himself helpless and completely dependent upon the care of two young humans. He grew up here. He got to know us at our level and on our turf. He left the comfort and grandeur of heaven behind. He experienced it all.

Has anyone ever tried to comfort you while you were hurting but had never been through your situation? It's nice to have someone who cares about you and can pray for you. But to have someone who has been there and gotten through it—that is life changing and more comforting than anything else. Jesus became one of us to offer comfort, hope, and eternal life from someone who has been there, overcome, and conquered!

Not man, who can be seen, should be followed, but God, who cannot be seen. So then, that we might be shown one who would be both seen and followed, God became man.

SAINT AUGUSTINE

It is not enough to believe theoretically that
[Jesus] was both God and Man; not enough to
admire, respect, and even worship Him; it is
not even enough to try to follow Him.
The reason for the insufficiency of these things
is that the modern intelligent mind, which
has had its horizons widened in dozens of
different ways, has got to be shocked afresh
by the audacious central fact. . .that, as a sober
matter of history, God became one of us.

J. B. PHILIPS

Shocked Afresh

❧

*In the days of his flesh, Jesus offered up
prayers and supplications, with loud cries
and tears, to him who was able to save him
from death, and he was heard because of his
reverence. Although he was a son, he learned
obedience through what he suffered. And
being made perfect, he became the source of
eternal salvation to all who obey him.*

HEBREWS 5:7–9 ESV

Your parents and grandparents have done their job if you've heard about the birth of Jesus your whole life. As Joel 1:3 says, "Tell it to your children, and let your children tell it to their children and their children to the next generation."

Hearing about the Christmas story is wonderful! The problem comes when we've heard it told in boring and lifeless ways over the years. Or as a cute little story we remember from Sunday school that hasn't really changed us at all.

Let Jesus' birth be more than just a story. Let it be more than a sweet nativity scene ooh-ed and aww-ed over during the holidays. As you tell the story to your friends, family, and children, tell it with great awe and reverence. Don't let the story become a boring paragraph read quickly before Christmas dinner. Let it change you every time you hear it.

Be shocked afresh.

Heavenly Father, help me humble myself and come to You always with faith like a child. Help me know and believe that You are the God of miracles—yesterday, today, and forever. Help me be shocked afresh by the powerful story of Your birth, Your life, Your death, and Your resurrection. As I share this story with my family and friends in the coming months and years, open their hearts to hear Your Word. Light up my heart, my face, and my words as I share the life-changing truth of the first Christmas.

As I really take the time to think about You—the God of all creation—becoming human, I'm thoroughly astonished. I cannot fathom it. How You could love me so much to leave Your throne room and become a helpless child. To grow up human when You knew that You were King of all is unbelievable, and yet I know in my heart it is true. How can I begin to say thanks? I hope the way I live my life is pleasing to You. It's the only way I know how to express my deepest thanks and praise for what You've done.

Let the Story Change You

❧

And now, just as you accepted Christ
Jesus as your Lord, you must continue
to follow him. Let your roots grow down
into him, and let your lives be built on him.
Then your faith will grow strong in the
truth you were taught, and you will
overflow with thankfulness.

COLOSSIANS 2:6-7

"Maybe Christmas doesn't come from a store," thought Dr. Seuss's Grinch. "Maybe Christmas. . .perhaps. . .means a little bit more."

You might be able to recite the Christmas story backward and forward, but have you let it change you? Is it more than a holiday tradition? Colossians 2:6-7 encourages us to let our roots grow deep in Christ after we've accepted Him as our Savior. We've got to let our lives be built on Him if the Christmas message is really going to matter.

This Christmas, thank the mentors and teachers you've had in your life—the ones who have taught you about faith year after year. Our faith can grow strong in the truths that we've been taught over the years by our parents and grandparents, our pastors and Sunday school teachers. Let it mean something. Let the stories change you. And Christmas will mean a whole lot more.

Survive and Thrive

❧

*Don't let anyone capture you with empty philoso-
phies and high-sounding nonsense that come from
human thinking and from the spiritual powers of
this world, rather than from Christ. For in Christ
lives all the fullness of God in a human body. So you
also are complete through your union with Christ,
who is the head over every ruler and authority.*

COLOSSIANS 2:8–10 NLT

"All roads lead to heaven." "No one is right or
wrong, they're just different." "There is a higher
power, but he or she just wants you to be
happy." Have you heard any of these? There are
many popular authors and speakers today who
are sucking millions of people into these par-
ticular lies. Paul warns us in Colossians to keep
away from philosophies and ideas that come
from humans and are in direct contradiction
to God's Word. What's scary is that they sound
so good to so many! Today's false teachers–
even some who are quoting the Bible–like to

slip in a little bit of truth with a whole bunch of nonsense that is against the Word of God. They think they are bringing people happiness and light, but in reality they are leading people away from God.

What does this have to do with Christmas? People are often vulnerable during the holidays. They are looking for life change and listening to whomever sounds good. Keep your eyes and ears open for friends and family who are being led astray by false teachings and mysticism. Let them know in loving ways that if what they're believing doesn't match up with God's words, they're headed for a dead end.

All the fullness of God abides in Christ Jesus—that's the truth of the incarnation. Your relationship with Christ is all you need to survive and thrive in this world.

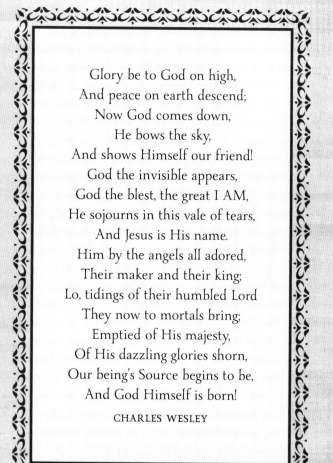

Glory be to God on high,
And peace on earth descend;
Now God comes down,
He bows the sky,
And shows Himself our friend!
God the invisible appears,
God the blest, the great I AM,
He sojourns in this vale of tears,
And Jesus is His name.
Him by the angels all adored,
Their maker and their king;
Lo, tidings of their humbled Lord
They now to mortals bring;
Emptied of His majesty,
Of His dazzling glories shorn,
Our being's Source begins to be,
And God Himself is born!

CHARLES WESLEY

In order that man might journey more trustfully toward the truth, the Truth itself, the Son of God, having assumed human nature, established and founded faith.

SAINT AUGUSTINE

An End to Sin's Control

❧

The law of Moses was unable to save us because of the weakness of our sinful nature. So God did what the law could not do. He sent his own Son in a body like the bodies we sinners have. And in that body God declared an end to sin's control over us by giving his Son as a sacrifice for our sins.

ROMANS 8:3 NLT

Romans 7:15–18 explains mankind's sinful nature well: "I do not understand what I do. For what I want to do I do not do, but what I hate I do. And if I do what I do not want to do, I agree that the law is good. As it is, it is no longer I myself who do it, but it is sin living in me. For I know that good itself does not dwell in me, that is, in my sinful nature. For I have the desire to do what is good, but I cannot carry it out."

Romans 8:3 tells us that God did what the law could never do. Knowing we could never measure up according to the law, God sent His own Son as our sacrifice. Love did what the law couldn't.

Consider the words of the late pastor and author Henry van Dyke: "Are you willing to believe that love is the strongest thing in the world—stronger than hate, stronger than evil, stronger than death—and that the blessed life which began in Bethlehem nineteen hundred years ago is the image and brightness of the Eternal Love? Then you can keep Christmas."

Are you keeping Christmas throughout the year? Do you believe the great importance of Jesus' birth? The incarnation was the beginning of the end of sin's control!

Lord, I confess I'm a little worried about strange beliefs I'm hearing from friends and family that don't quite match up with Your Word. Please give me wisdom and discernment as I share truth with them. If it is Your will that I speak up about these issues, please open the doors wide for me to have such a conversation. Please give me the words to say so that they don't feel I am judging or condemning them but speaking to them out of love and concern for their well-being. Help me not to worry and help me trust that You will lead me.

Heavenly Father, please go before me throughout all the upcoming family gatherings, Christmas events, activities, and holiday festivities.
I'll see so many friends and family this month.
Some know and love You and others don't. Help
me not to be shy about my love for You and the
awesome truth of Your incarnation. Continue
to open doors for spiritual conversations so that
I can share my love for You. I know my actions
often speak louder than my words, so please
help me live out my faith each day.

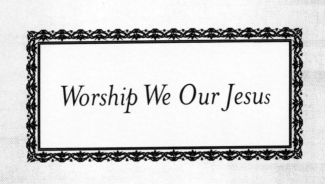

Worship We Our Jesus

Waiting and Worship

❦

And Mary said, "My soul magnifies the Lord,
and my spirit rejoices in God my Savior, for he
has looked on the humble estate of his servant.
For behold, from now on all generations will call
me blessed; for he who is mighty has done great
things for me, and holy is his name."

LUKE 1:46–49 ESV

Nobody particularly *likes* to wait. As young
Mary waited for the birth of her son she worshipped God. She was afraid at first, but God
spoke to her heart. He knew she was fully His.
He knew she would answer the call and follow
His will. Mary allowed God to completely
disrupt all her plans, and she did so without
throwing a fit. Instead she worshipped.

How many of us worship God while we
wait? Chances are we'll have a lot of waiting
to do before Christmas. When you find yourself stuck in a never-ending line at the mall or
caught in the middle of a traffic jam, don't get
upset. Worship. Thank God for all His blessings

to you. Pray for each member of your family. Pray for friends and family members who don't know God personally. Pray for the frustrated cashier at the counter. Psalm 37:7 says, "Be still before the lord and wait patiently for him." When your plans are messed up this Christmas—and some of them probably will be—take time to get your focus off yourself and your circumstances and just worship the Lord.

A Life of Worship

❦

In the sixth month of Elizabeth's pregnancy,
God sent the angel Gabriel to Nazareth,
a town in Galilee, to a virgin pledged to
be married to a man named Joseph, a
descendant of David. The virgin's name
was Mary. The angel went to her and said,
"Greetings, you who are highly favored!
The Lord is with you."

LUKE 1:26–28

*D*id you ever wonder why God chose Mary? A young girl that nobody particularly knew about. She wasn't famous. She didn't have a blog or a Facebook page with a huge following. She wasn't a talented author or speaker. She was just Mary. A simple girl who loved God. Yet she became God's chosen one. The one who would carry and nurture His Son. The one who would teach God to talk and eat solid food and subtract.

God can use anyone who says simply, "I'm Yours, Lord. I'll do what You say." This is what God wants to hear from His children. When you live a life of worship, you open the doors for God to do amazing things with your life. He will use you in ways that you may never know or understand until heaven.

In the quiet of your heart this Christmas, whisper these words to your Creator: "I'm Yours, Lord. I'll do what You say. I want to live a life of worship. Use me."

Angels from the realms of glory,
Wing your flight o'er all the earth;
Ye who sang creation's story
Now proclaim Messiah's birth.
Come and worship, come and worship,
Worship Christ, the newborn King.

Shepherds, in the field abiding,
Watching o'er your flocks by night,
God with us is now residing;
Yonder shines the infant light.
Come and worship, come and worship,
Worship Christ, the newborn King.

JAMES MONTGOMERY

What can I give Him, poor as I am?
If I were a shepherd I would bring a lamb.
If I were a wise man I would do my part.
Yet what can I give Him?
Give Him my heart.

CHRISTINA ROSSETTI

The Christmas Message

Mary was greatly troubled at his words and wondered what kind of greeting this might be. But the angel said to her, "Do not be afraid, Mary; you have found favor with God. You will conceive and give birth to a son, and you are to call him Jesus. He will be great and will be called the Son of the Most High. The Lord God will give him the throne of his father David, and he will reign over Jacob's descendants forever; his kingdom will never end."

LUKE 1:29–33

J. I. Packer said, "The Christmas message is that there is hope for a ruined humanity–hope of pardon, hope of peace with God, hope of glory–because at the Father's will, Jesus became poor and was born in a stable so that thirty years later He might hang on a cross."

We worship God for who He is and for all that He has done. He is our Creator, our Savior, our Sustainer, and our Friend. He brought hope to a ruined humanity. And the stark truth of the Christmas message is that the baby Jesus was born. . .to die. While the birth of Jesus is looked at with awe and wonder, it was also the beginning of the end. The baby was born with a great purpose.

As Jesus grew into a man, He knew what was coming. And yet He loved deeply, without hesitation. He knew His friends and family would betray Him, but He kept loving them and pointing them to the truth. He knew they would never understand until His resurrection, when they saw His nail-pierced hands.

The Christmas message is about the cross. Jesus was born to die for you.

Psalm 63 is my prayer today as I worship You, heavenly Father: "O God, you are my God; I earnestly search for you. My soul thirsts for you; my whole body longs for you in this parched and weary land where there is no water. I have seen you in your sanctuary and gazed upon your power and glory. Your unfailing love is better than life itself; how I praise you! I will praise you as long as I live, lifting up my hands to you in prayer. You satisfy me more than the richest feast. I will praise you with songs of joy" (Psalm 63:1-5 NLT).

Dear God, help me live a life of worship and give You glory for who You are. Let my heart be full of love for You. Just as Mary did, let me live a life that pleases You. I commit myself fully to Your plans and purposes for me. Please remove any selfishness in me. I'm Yours, Lord. I'll do what You say. I want to live a life of worship. Use me.

Nothing Is Impossible with God

❦

"How will this be," Mary asked the angel, "since I am a virgin?" The angel answered, "The Holy Spirit will come on you, and the power of the Most High will overshadow you. So the holy one to be born will be called the Son of God. Even Elizabeth your relative is going to have a child in her old age, and she who was said to be unable to conceive is in her sixth month. For no word from God will ever fail."

LUKE 1:34–37

What a wonderful time of the year to be reminded that our God is the God of the impossible! Nothing—absolutely nothing—is impossible when God is behind it! Are you facing some difficult situations this season? Are you hurting over a broken relationship? Are you weary or afraid or alone? God can take all the broken pieces of your life and make something beautiful out of them—if you're willing!

Often family issues arise around the holidays. The stress of the season can cause personalities to clash and bring out the worst in us if we aren't careful. Pray for your family. Pray that God would mend any broken relationships. Listen for God's prompting. If you have family members who are hard to get along with, go to them and talk things through. Our great God can heal even the most difficult and seemingly irreparable relationships!

The Lord's Servant

❧

"I am the Lord's servant," Mary answered.
"May your word to me be fulfilled."
Then the angel left her.

LUKE 1:38

Glory to God in the highest!" If we, like Mary, are daily praising God and our hearts are full of love for Him, others cannot help but see the difference He has made in our lives! Worship isn't just about singing songs or Christmas carols at church on Sundays. It's about living life in such a way that is pleasing to God. If we are living a life of worship, we cannot help but tell others about who He is and what He has done for us.

Our God is the Lord of heaven and earth. God's Word says that He doesn't live in temples built by human hands. He is the living God who resides in our hearts. He doesn't need us to serve Him, but He wants us to. We shouldn't serve Him because we feel guilty. Instead, we should serve Him as an act of worship to the God who gave us life and breath and everything else (Acts 17:24–28). Whether it is serving as a prayer partner at church, rocking babies in the nursery, welcoming people as they walk into the worship center, playing the keyboard for the worship team, or serving a meal at the local soup kitchen, there is a place for everyone to serve!

Hark! the herald angels sing,
"Glory to the newborn King;
Peace on earth, and mercy mild,
God and sinners reconciled!"
Joyful, all ye nations rise,
Join the triumph of the skies;
With th'angelic host proclaim,
"Christ is born in Bethlehem!" . . .

Hark! the herald angels sing,
"Glory to the newborn King!"
Christ, by highest Heav'n adored;
Christ the everlasting Lord;
Late in time, behold Him come,
Offspring of a virgin's womb.
Veiled in flesh the Godhead see;
Hail th'incarnate Deity.
Pleased with us in flesh to dwell,
Jesus our Emmanuel.
Hark! the herald angels sing,
"Glory to the newborn King!"

CHARLES WESLEY

Worship No Matter What

❧

*"His mercy extends to those who fear him, from
generation to generation. He has performed mighty
deeds with his arm; he has scattered those who are
proud in their inmost thoughts. He has brought
down rulers from their thrones but has lifted up
the humble. He has filled the hungry with good
things but has sent the rich away empty. He has
helped his servant Israel, remembering to be
merciful to Abraham and his descendants forever,
just as he promised our ancestors."*

LUKE 1:50–55

Stop and think about all that God has done
for you. Consider starting your own faith jour-
nal to write those thoughts in. If you're not the
journaling type, just keep a notebook handy to
jot down occasional prayers and things you'd
like to remember about your relationship
with God. Start by listing the blessings you
have experienced during your lifetime. List the
hurts, too, and how God comforted you and

sustained you. Write down why God is worthy of your worship.

Do you ever go out of your way to worship the Lord? Do you worship even when it isn't convenient for you? God is worthy of our worship whether we feel like worshipping or not. If you've had a rough week, aren't feeling well, or are stressed about something, remember that God is still worthy of your worship. When we worship God even when we don't feel like it, our focus shifts from ourselves to the Lord and our problems look much smaller in His presence! Keep track of how God has been faithful to you. Then when you don't feel much like worshipping, you can look back and see why He's still worthy of your worship no matter what.

Heavenly Father, sometimes I feel like the persistent widow You mention in the Bible. The one who kept going to the judge about the same thing over and over again. And sometimes I get tired of praying because I feel like nothing is happening. I don't feel very much like worshipping. Please change my heart and my attitude. I know You hear my prayer, and I trust that You will do what is best for me. Help me not to lose heart but to remember Your love and faithfulness.

Dear God, help me worship You even when I don't feel like it. You are worthy of all my worship, all the time! I lose my perspective too often. I take my eyes off You for a moment and then all of my troubles look bigger than they are. Forgive me for my selfishness. Cleanse me from my sin and help me get my focus back on You. Help me worship You with my whole life, with everything I am.

*Love Shall
Be Our Token*

A Keepsake

❧

But Mary treasured up all these things
and pondered them in her heart. The
shepherds returned, glorifying and praising
God for all the things they had heard and seen,
which were just as they had been told.

LUKE 2:19–20

It comes every year and will go on forever. And along with Christmas belong the keepsakes and the customs. Those humble, everyday things a mother clings to, and ponders, like Mary in the secret spaces of her heart." This quote by the late inspirational author Marjorie Holmes gives a glimpse inside a mother's heart at Christmas.

Baby's first Christmas is a big deal. T-shirts are printed, ornaments are customized, and Santa hats are embroidered to keep record of this momentous occasion because all mothers know that children don't stay little for long. The wrapping paper and boxes won't be nearly as exciting next year as they are to a baby this year.

Mary didn't have any of these extravagances for Jesus. She didn't even get to take a picture of her precious baby lying in a manger. Instead, she treasured every moment. She pondered them in her heart and kept the love she felt as her keepsake.

Live in the moment this holiday season. Treasure each event, occasion, and moment as it comes. Slow down and feel the love in your heart. Remember it. Take great pleasure in watching children smile and get excited about every little thing. Watch for the twinkle in the eyes of your friends and family. Ponder the love you all share.

Love shall be our keepsake.

The Treasure

We now have this light shining in our hearts, but we ourselves are like fragile clay jars containing this great treasure. This makes it clear that our great power is from God, not from ourselves.

2 CORINTHIANS 4:7 NLT

More light than we can learn,
More wealth than we can treasure,
More love than we can earn,
More peace than we can measure,
Because one Child is born.

CHRISTOPHER FRY

One child brought light, unmeasured wealth, love, and peace to all mankind. This unmeasured wealth, this great treasure, is the light that shines in our hearts. The Bible says that we humans are just fragile jars of clay containing this great light. But that's what makes it clear to everyone what a miracle it is! The great power and treasure we have inside us is Christ Himself! He inhabits our souls through the Holy Spirit that God sent.

God wants us to be fully aware that His power and presence are available to us as we go through every moment of life. He created us to have an eternal relationship with Him. Even though our containers are fragile, God's power enables us to do all things through Christ who gives us strength (Philippians 4:13).

Take note of this truth: "The lord is my rock, my fortress, and my savior; my God is my rock, in whom I find protection. He is my shield, the power that saves me, and my place of safety" (Psalm 18:2 NLT). There is no greater treasure!

What Child is this who, laid to rest
On Mary's lap, is sleeping?
Whom angels greet with anthems sweet,
While shepherds watch are keeping?
This, this is Christ the King,
Whom shepherds guard and angels sing;
Haste, haste, to bring Him laud,
The Babe, the Son of Mary...

So bring Him incense, gold, and myrrh,
Come peasant, king to own Him;
The King of kings salvation brings,
Let loving hearts enthrone Him.
Raise, raise a song on high,
The virgin sings her lullaby.
Joy, joy for Christ is born,
The Babe, the Son of Mary.

WILLIAM C. DIX

I'm so amazed that Your presence is available to me, that the power of Your Spirit lives inside me to whisper Your truth and comfort to me at all times. What an incredible blessing! What an unmatched treasure! You are the Potter, and I am the clay. I pray that You would mold me into something useful in Your hands. Allow me to live in the moment. As I go through Christmas and the days to come, help me enjoy each and every situation. Let me soak in the moments and cherish the time You've given me with my loved ones.

Heavenly Father, I believe what the Bible says in Matthew 6:21: "Where your treasure is, there your heart will be also." I don't want to get caught up in earthly treasures. I don't want my "stuff" to hold high priority. Help me to be a good steward of all you've blessed me with, but let my heart hold eternal things in utmost regard. I long for an eternal perspective in all things. I pray that You would help me see Your plans and purposes in everything. Let the love of Christ be my token, my keepsake, and my guide.

Delight in the Almighty

❧

*"If you give up your lust for money and throw
your precious gold into the river, the Almighty
himself will be your treasure. He will be your
precious silver! Then you will take delight in
the Almighty and look up to God."*

JOB 22:24–26 NLT

On a couple of days another Christmas will
be over. Decorations will be taken down and
the grind of daily life will resume. We must do
something to remember that the message and
meaning of Christmas does not cease when
the celebration is over. Christmas is not really
about a celebration, Christmas trees, and piles of
gifts. Christmas, the coming of Christ, is about
everyday life. God is with us, and we need to do
anything we can to remember that fact the rest
of the year." In this quote, Pastor Bruce Goett-
sche makes it clear that the meaning of Christmas must be remembered all year long.

Job 22:24–26 reminds us to give up our
desire for earthly treasures and worthless

material possessions and take delight in God Himself. We need to let Him be our treasure at Christmas and the whole year long. Psalm 37:4 says to "Take delight in the Lord, and he will give you the desires of your heart."

What can you and your family do to remember and keep Christmas the whole year through? Consider sitting down as a family to discuss this. Talk about the importance of not letting the birth of Christ become just another story. Discuss ways to delight in the Lord and live out the hope and love of Christmas every day.

The Wondrous Gift

❧

My son, if you receive my words and treasure up
my commandments with you, making your ear
attentive to wisdom and inclining your heart to
understanding; yes, if you call out for insight and
raise your voice for understanding, if you seek it like
silver and search for it as for hidden treasures,
then you will understand the fear of the Lord
and find the knowledge of God.

PROVERBS 2:1–5 ESV

To fear God simply means that you recognize
God's power and that you strive to follow His
commands. It means you seek after Him like
you would a valuable treasure, a wondrous gift.

Author Frank McKibben said it well: "This
is Christmas: not the tinsel, not the giving and
receiving, not even the carols, but the humble
heart that receives anew the wondrous gift, the
Christ."

In Romans 5:15–16 Paul writes, "But there
is a great difference between Adam's sin and

God's gracious gift. For the sin of this one man, Adam, brought death to many. But even greater is God's wonderful grace and his gift of forgiveness to many through this other man, Jesus Christ. And the result of God's gracious gift is very different from the result of that one man's sin. For Adam's sin led to condemnation, but God's free gift leads to our being made right with God, even though we are guilty of many sins" (NLT).

God's great gift, the wondrous gift of His Son, allows us to be made right with God. His love is the greatest gift of all. Don't let that be cliché. Let it soak into your soul this holiday season.

He left His Father's throne above,
So free, so infinite His grace—
Emptied Himself of all but love,
And bled for Adam's helpless race.
'Tis mercy all, immense and free,
For O my God, it found out me!
'Tis mercy all, immense and free,
For O my God, it found out me! . . .

No condemnation now I dread;
Jesus, and all in Him, is mine.
Alive in Him, my living Head,
And clothed in righteousness divine,
Bold I approach th'eternal throne,
And claim the crown, through Christ my own.
Bold I approach th'eternal throne,
And claim the crown, through Christ my own.

Amazing love! How can it be,
That Thou, my God, shouldst die for me?

CHARLES WESLEY

Eternal Treasures

❧

They are to do good, to be rich in good
works, to be generous and ready to share,
thus storing up treasure for themselves as a
good foundation for the future, so that they
may take hold of that which is truly life.

1 TIMOTHY 6:18–19 ESV

Civil rights leader and author Howard Thurman gives us a good reminder concerning keeping Christmas all year long: "When the song of the angels is stilled, when the star in the sky is gone, when the kings and princes are home, when the shepherds are back with their flock, the work of Christmas begins: to find the lost, to heal the broken, to feed the hungry, to release the prisoner, to rebuild the nations, to bring peace among others, to make music in the heart."

Christmas is about giving from the heart. God gave us His Son! Let's give of ourselves to one another as an act of worship to our heavenly Father. Take some time with your family to think about what you can do for someone else this holiday season. Begin your December with the spirit of giving and cultivate it as much as possible throughout the month. Decide to bless someone in need. Give to the poor. Sponsor a child from a third-world country. Send a shoebox full of gifts to a child who has never experienced Christmas.

Presents and parties are fun for a while, but the true spirit of giving lasts for eternity.

Father, allow us to honor You in all that we do this season. Let us bless someone else in need this Christmas for the purpose of glorifying Your name. Thank You for the financial blessings You have given us. Help us to give back in a way that pleases You. Lead us to a person or a group of people that need our help. And please give us the willingness, ability, and resources to do whatever we can to meet their needs.

Dear Lord, please give my family a glimpse into Your heart. Let them be willing to have less this year so that we can bless others. Help us to embrace a giving spirit in our home. Let Your love guide us as we make financial decisions this holiday season. Teach us how to serve others with a grateful heart. Let us be content with what You've already blessed us with and not worried about always having the newest and best. Thank You for Your great gift to us, Jesus. Let that always be enough.

*Love to God and
All Men*

Love God, Love Others

❧

*One of the teachers of religious law was standing
there listening to the debate. He realized that Jesus
had answered well, so he asked, "Of all the
commandments, which is the most important?"
Jesus replied, "The most important commandment
is this: 'Listen, O Israel! The LORD our God is the
one and only LORD. And you must love the LORD
your God with all your heart, all your soul, all your
mind, and all your strength.' The second is equally
important: 'Love your neighbor as yourself.'
No other commandment is greater than these."*

MARK 12:28–31 NLT

Love to God and to all men. Jesus summed
up the entire law by saying our purpose in life
is twofold: love God and love others. Christmas
means a lot of things to a lot of people, but as
George F. McDougall said, "Best of all, Christmas means a spirit of love, a time when the
love of God and love of our fellow men should
prevail over all hatred and bitterness, a time

when our thoughts and deeds and the spirit of our lives manifest the presence of God."

Not everyone feels this way. But even those who are far from God, even those who don't understand or believe in the true meaning of Christmas, seem to wake up on Christmas morning and think, *"It's Christmas. I'm going to set aside my problems and anger for this one day and show love."*

Hearts tend to be a bit softer on Christmas. Pray for friends and family members whose hearts are softened. Ask God to be close to them and reveal Himself to them in very real ways.

Serve and Love

❧

*You, my brothers and sisters, were
called to be free. But do not use your
freedom to indulge the flesh; rather, serve
one another humbly in love. For the entire
law is fulfilled in keeping this one command:
"Love your neighbor as yourself."*

GALATIANS 5:13–14 NIV

It is Christmas every time you let God love others through you. . .yes, it is Christmas every time you smile at your brother and offer him your hand." Mother Teresa understood the true spirit of Christmas. She lived Christmas well as she loved and served God and others.

Mark 10:45 says, "For even the Son of Man did not come to be served, but to serve, and to give his life as a ransom for many." Jesus, the King of all kings, didn't come to earth to be served, although He deserved that. Rather, He came to serve and sacrifice. He lived a life of love, laying down His life to serve others.

Christianity isn't as complicated as man makes it. Jesus told us over and over again in the Gospels to love God and to love others:

"You have heard that it was said, 'Love your neighbor and hate your enemy.' But I tell you, Love your enemies and pray for those who persecute you" (Matthew 5:43–44).

"Love your neighbor as yourself" (Matthew 19:19).

That's the message of Christianity. That's the message of Christmas.

Joy to the world, the Lord is come!
Let earth receive her King;
Let every heart prepare Him room,
And Heaven and nature sing,
And Heaven and nature sing,
And Heaven, and Heaven,
and nature sing.

Joy to the earth, the Savior reigns!
Let men their songs employ;
While fields and floods,
rocks, hills, and plains
Repeat the sounding joy,
Repeat the sounding joy,
Repeat, repeat, the sounding joy.

ISAAC WATTS

Somehow, not only for Christmas,
But all the long year through,
The joy that you give to others,
Is the joy that comes back to you.

JOHN GREENLEAF WHITTIER

Joyful, Joy-full

"If you keep my commandments, you will abide in my love, just as I have kept my Father's commandments and abide in his love. These things I have spoken to you, that my joy may be in you, and that your joy may be full."

JOHN 15:10–11 ESV

Christmas is an entire season of hope, love, and joy—joy to the world! From unbelievers we often hear the phrase "Christmas is just for children." But that is simply untrue. Christmas is for all mankind. Jesus came to bring true joy to everyone. Joy that comes from knowing His love for us and the hope that truth brings. Even during difficult and dark times, we can remain in Christ's love and experience the joy of knowing Him.

Ponder the following scriptures regarding true and lasting joy:

You have turned my mourning into joyful dancing. You have taken away my clothes of mourning and clothed me with joy, that I might sing praises to you and not be silent. O Lord my God, I will give you thanks forever.

PSALM 30:11–12 NLT

But may the righteous be glad and rejoice before God; may they be happy and joyful.

PSALM 68:3 NIV

Satisfy us in the morning with your unfailing love, that we may sing for joy and be glad all our days.

PSALM 90:14 NIV

When anxiety was great within me, your consolation brought me joy.

PSALM 94:19 NIV

Joyful, joyful we adore Thee! Thank You, Jesus, for true and lasting joy that comes from You alone!

Father, this is my prayer today. As Christmas approaches, drive doubt away and fill me with Your light. I worship You with joy because of the hope and love You have brought me. Let me live that I might praise You (Psalm 119:175).

Heavenly Father, I'm excited that love is in the air at Christmas. I find it a bit easier to see others through Your eyes during the holidays. Give me an opportunity to fully express my love to those closest to me and to share Your love with the people who need it most. Thank You that You've simplified Your message to us. Help me wrap my brain around the fact that all I need to do is love You and love others. I don't need to remember a list of rules and worry that I'm messing up all the time. I just need to love.

Our Gift to God

❦

Therefore, I urge you, brothers and sisters, in view of God's mercy, to offer your bodies as a living sacrifice, holy and pleasing to God—this is your true and proper worship. Do not conform to the pattern of this world, but be transformed by the renewing of your mind. Then you will be able to test and approve what God's will is—his good, pleasing and perfect will.

ROMANS 12:1–2

*O*ur gift to God is becoming a living sacrifice. But what is a living sacrifice? It is a daily surrendering of our will and our desires for God's. It is a life of everyday worship where we are constantly seeking to serve and love God and others. To be willing to be and do whatever He asks of us at any given moment. This says "thank You" to God more than words ever could. This is the gift God wants from each of us. A great big daily "thank You" expressing itself in the way we live our lives.

Perhaps the late pastor and author Dr. Vance Havner said it best: "Christmas is based on an exchange of gifts, the gift of God to man—His unspeakable gift of His Son, and the gift of man to God—when we present our bodies a living sacrifice."

Christmas-only Worship

❧

I love you, LORD; you are my strength.
The LORD is my rock, my fortress, and my
savior; my God is my rock, in whom I find
protection. He is my shield, the power that
saves me, and my place of safety. I called
on the LORD, who is worthy of praise,
and he saved me from my enemies.

PSALM 18:1–3 NLT

Churches are often full of Sunday-only worshippers. Especially at Christmas. The ones that pretend to love God on Sundays but disregard Him the rest of the week, or even the rest of the year! They want to be seen at church on Christmas, but come New Year's Day they are back to living for themselves. Jesus says that

those people honor Him with their lips,
but their hearts are actually far from God
(Matthew 15:8).

Are you honoring God with your lips?
That's great! But make sure your heart is in
it, too. God wants us to live our lives in true,
everyday worship. This is a daily laying down
of your own selfish desires and following after
Christ. This is viewing the mundane tasks of
life as acts of service to God. (Yep, doing the
laundry, taking the car to the shop, and sending
an e-mail can be acts of worship to God when
done in the right spirit!) This is accepting each
challenge and blessing with grace and recogniz-
ing God's hand in the midst of it all.

Don't be just a Christmas worshipper. Live
every day as an act of worship.

Come, Thou long expected Jesus
Born to set Thy people free;
From our fears and sins release us,
Let us find our rest in Thee.
Israel's strength and consolation,
Hope of all the earth Thou art;
Dear desire of every nation,
Joy of every longing heart. . .

Born Thy people to deliver,
Born a child and yet a King,
Born to reign in us forever,
Now Thy gracious kingdom bring.
By Thine own eternal Spirit
Rule in all our hearts alone;
By Thine all sufficient merit,
Raise us to Thy glorious throne.

CHARLES WESLEY

Remember!

❦

*"But I have this complaint against you.
You don't love me or each other as you did
at first! Look how far you have fallen! Turn
back to me and do the works you did at first."*

REVELATION 2:4–5 NLT

Look around you at church this Christmas.
See all the new and old faces scrambling to get
a seat before the service begins, dressed in their
best. It's almost like the whole world remembers,
for one day, that Christmas is about Jesus and
maybe they should come and worship Him.

Former *New York Times* writer Lucinda
Franks made this comment: "Christmas in
Bethlehem. The ancient dream: a cold, clear
night made brilliant by a glorious star, the
smell of incense, shepherds and wise men falling to their knees in adoration of the sweet
baby, the incarnation of perfect love." The first
Christmas is like an ancient dream. But it is
also a dream come true. Can you remember
back to the first time you heard the Christmas

story? Can you recall when and where you first heard about Christ and all that He came to do for you? Was there ever a time in your life when you literally fell to your knees in adoration of Jesus?

Take the time to think back about your relationship with Christ and when it first began. Let the memories stir your heart. Ask God to remind you of His faithfulness and love. Ask Him to rekindle the fire that once burned in your heart for Him.

Remember your first love! Remember!

O Lord, You have examined my heart and know everything about me. You know when I sit down or stand up. You know my thoughts even when I'm far away. You see me when I travel and when I rest at home. You know everything I do. You know what I am going to say even before I say it, Lord. You go before me and follow me. You place your hand of blessing on my head (Psalm 139:1–5). I praise You and thank You for Your great love for me.

Forgive me, Father, for falling away from You.
I'm sorry that I'm not as enthusiastic about my
faith as I was when I first came to know You.
Life has gotten in the way, and I've allowed that
to happen. I've felt out of touch with You,
and I know that I'm the one who has walked away
from our relationship. Bring me back to You.
I want to rediscover Your plans for my life.
I want to be completely sold out to You.
You are my first love. Help me remember.

Love for Plea and Gift and Sign

No Greater Love

❧

*"This is my commandment, that you
love one another as I have loved you.
Greater love has no one than this, that
someone lay down his life for his friends."*

JOHN 15:12–13 ESV

Think of all the Christmas movies you've seen
in your lifetime. On Christmas day, the charac-
ters generally wake up with a smile. They have
joy in their hearts. Their hearts are filled with
love for others. Even if they don't know that
true love was born in a baby that first Christmas in Bethlehem thousands of years before.

Charles Dickens said, "I have always thought of Christmas time as a good time; a kind, forgiving, charitable, pleasant time; the only time I know of in the long calendar of the year, when men and women seem by one consent to open their shut-up hearts freely."

Ecclesiastes 3:11 tells us "[God] has made everything beautiful in its time. He has also set eternity in the human heart; yet no one can fathom what God has done from beginning to end." God set eternity in our hearts. It's almost like there is a vacuum inside that can never be filled until we find the love of Christ. And maybe we're just more likely to accept that love at Christmastime.

Jesus wants us to love as He loved. To be willing to lay down our lives for the sake of others. Let the world see Jesus through *you* this Christmas. Love as He loved.

Eternal Things

❧

*"You did not choose me, but I chose
you and appointed you that you should
go and bear fruit and that your fruit
should abide, so that whatever you ask
the Father in my name, he may give
it to you. These things I command you,
so that you will love one another."*

JOHN 15:16–17 ESV

Fruit baskets are a common and festive gift at Christmas. The next time you see one, remember the verses in John 15. How are you doing at bearing fruit for Christ? Are you doing a good job of showing love to everyone in your life? J. C. Penney said, "Christmas is not just a time for festivity and merry making. It is more than that. It is a time for the contemplation of eternal things. The Christmas spirit is a spirit of giving and forgiving."

This December, set up a family night and read John 15 together. Make the night festive and merry, but also use it as a time to contemplate eternal things. Find a recipe for a new dessert made with fruit. Use the dessert as an illustration of the message in John 15. Discuss true love and what it means to abide in Christ. Ask your family to evaluate how effectively each of you is living for Christ. Pray for God to lead you into the New Year following His plan and purpose for your family in a spirit of giving and forgiving.

Thou didst leave Thy throne
and Thy kingly crown,
When Thou camest to earth for me;
But in Bethlehem's home was
there found no room
For Thy holy nativity.

O come to my heart, Lord Jesus,
There is room in my heart for Thee...

Heaven's arches rang when the angels sang,
Proclaiming Thy royal degree;
But of lowly birth didst Thou come to earth,
And in great humility.

O come to my heart, Lord Jesus,
There is room in my heart for Thee.

EMILY E. S. ELLIOTT

Jesus, I understand that Christmas is about love. Your love for me and for all mankind. I want to honor the season and purpose of Christmas all year long. Help me to use the simple truths of Christmastime in every season. I see Christmas in the smiles of men, women, and children quite a bit in December. I wish those smiles would last on their faces all year long. Help me encourage the Spirit of love in everyone I see.

Thank You, Father, for the great and wondrous gift of Jesus. As this season comes to a close and a new year begins, talk show hosts, celebrities, and health experts will urge us to overcome whatever struggles we have faced this past year. What a great hope and relief it is to me that all I need to do is trust in Your faithfulness and cast all my cares upon You, knowing that You have overcome the world. I lay all my burdens at Your feet, and I look forward to the new year ahead.

Love, Just Love

❧

*"A new commandment I give to you,
that you love one another: just as I
have loved you, you also are to love
one another. By this all people will know
that you are my disciples, if you have
love for one another."*

JOHN 13:34–35 ESV

Christmas means something. Love is in the
air at Christmas. Believers or not. God created every human being and gave each of us a
choice to love Him. Hamilton Wright Mabie
said, "Blessed is the season which engages the
whole world in a conspiracy of love."

If you get nothing else from this book, get

this: Christmas is about love. Love came down at Christmas. Love is what will draw even the hardest of hearts to search for a God they do not yet know. God uses those of us that believe in Him and follow Him to carry out His plans here on earth. Choose to love. In every relationship and situation that God allows to come your way, you have a choice. You can choose to respond with love or without. The world is full of difficult, unreasonable people who will, at times, get in your face and cause you pain. Can you respond in love?

Yes. By the power of the Holy Spirit, Jesus' love abides in you and gives you the ability to choose love. This doesn't mean that you are a doormat. Jesus was never portrayed in that way. He was a strong servant-leader who loved and spoke truth to all. Ask Him to fill you with His love and wisdom so that you can choose to love even the unlovable—and draw hardened hearts to seek His face.

A Spark and a Promise

*"For the Father himself loves you, because
you have loved me and have believed that I
came from God. I came from the Father and
have come into the world, and now I am leaving
the world and going to the Father. . . . I have said
these things to you, that in me you may have peace.
In the world you will have tribulation. But take
heart; I have overcome the world."*

JOHN 16:27–28, 33 ESV

William Law, an eighteenth-century theologian said, "When therefore the first spark of a desire after God arises in thy soul, cherish it with all thy care, give all thy heart into it; it is nothing less than a touch of the divine loadstone, that is to draw thee out of the vanity of time, into the riches of eternity. Get up, therefore, and follow it as gladly as the wise men of the east followed the star from heaven that appeared to them. It will do for thee as the star did for them, it will lead thee to the birth of

Jesus, not in a stable at Bethlehem in Judea, but to the birth of Jesus in the dark center of thine own soul."

When you first invite the spark of Christ's light into your soul, nourish it, chase after it, never let the spark die. Jesus came, died, and rose again to show us eternal love and give us peace on earth—and for all eternity. We're still here for a while to do His will. To love others and lead them to Him.

But Jesus gave us a promise: "I will see you again, and your hearts will rejoice, and no one will take your joy from you" (John 16:22 ESV).

Love came down at Christmas with a spark of light for us all and a magnificent promise. While we wait for God's purposes to be fulfilled, remember to keep Christmas everyday—and keep it well!

About the Author

MariLee Parrish lives in Ohio with her husband, Eric, and young children. She's a speaker, musician, and writer who desires to paint a picture of God with her life, talents, and ministries. Visit her website at www.marileeparrish.com for more info.